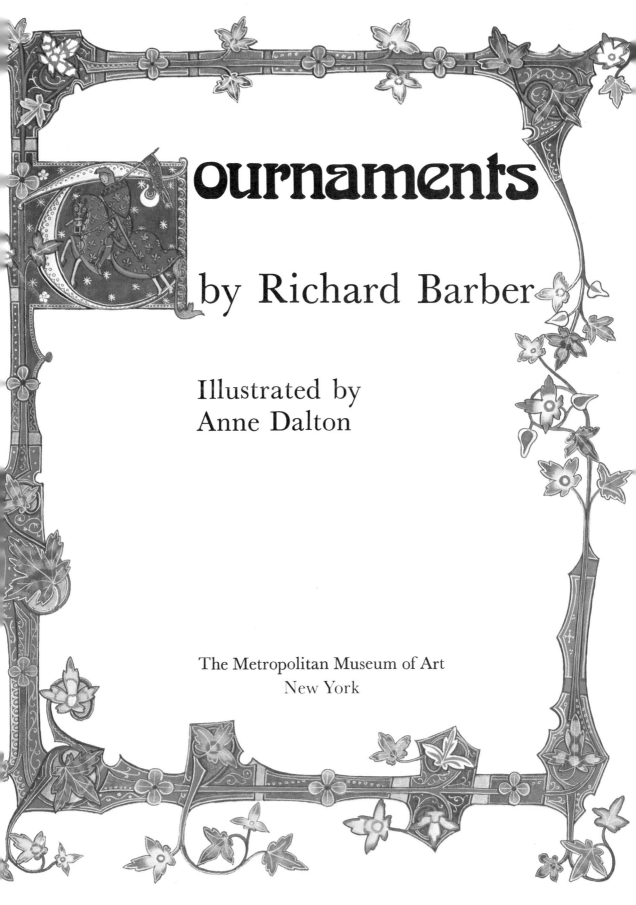

Tournaments

by Richard Barber

Illustrated by
Anne Dalton

The Metropolitan Museum of Art
New York

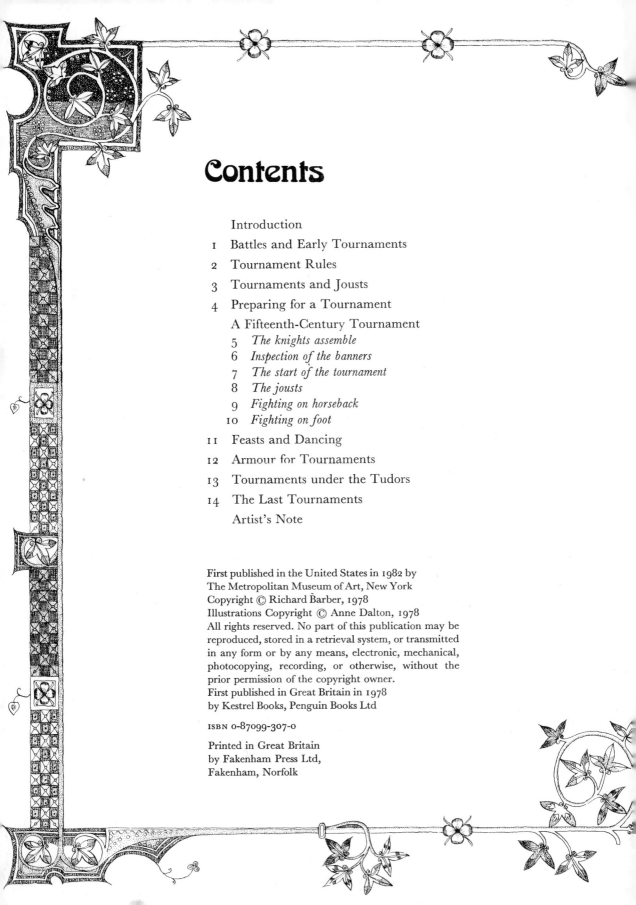

Contents

First published in the United States in 1982 by
The Metropolitan Museum of Art, New York
Copyright © Richard Barber, 1978
Illustrations Copyright © Anne Dalton, 1978

First published in Great Britain in 1978
by Kestrel Books, Penguin Books Ltd

ISBN 0-87099-307-0

Printed in Great Britain
by Fakenham Press Ltd,
Fakenham, Norfolk

Introduction

In the Middle Ages, armies were made up of knights, who fought on horseback, and ordinary soldiers, who fought on foot. Ordinary soldiers wore simple armour and carried simple weapons, and they needed little training unless they were archers and used a crossbow or a longbow. Up and down England men practised archery on the village greens, and held competitions to test their skill.

The knight needed much more complicated skills. He had to be able to manage his horse properly, even though he was wearing armour, and he had to be able to use a spear and sword at the same time. Like the archers, knights held competitions to test their skill, and it is these events, called tournaments, that this book is about.

The earliest tournaments were held about the middle of the eleventh century, and there were still tournaments of a kind as late as 1620. So it is not surprising that they changed considerably over such a length of time. The tournament we are going to describe dates from about 1450, when the rules for such events had been carefully worked out, but to understand it properly we must start with the way real wars were fought.

A knight was brought up to believe that individual courage was the most important thing in life: if he wanted to win fame, it would be by some great 'feat of arms', a brave deed on the battlefield. Now most wars consisted of skirmishes, involving only a few knights, and raids or sieges, aimed at destroying the enemy's lands or capturing his towns. None of these were particularly heroic. Skirmishes and ambushes might give a knight a chance to show off his personal bravery, but raiding was mostly a matter of burning defenceless people's houses; sieges meant camping for months outside a town while engineers tried to tunnel under the walls or build towers so that the besiegers could get over them. The knight only had a chance to show his prowess in the actual attack, which might last a few hours at the most. Battles, in which every knight hoped to take part, were very rare events.

1 Battles and Early Tournaments

The most famous battles were the really dramatic ones like Poitiers, where the Black Prince captured the King of France in 1356, or Agincourt, where Henry V defeated the French in 1415. Every knight dreamed of being on the winning side in such a battle. And even if he was on the losing side, the chances of his being injured or killed were not all that great, because any knight who was captured could be made to pay for his freedom. This was called 'ransoming', and it made war a kind of formal game for knights. Only the foot-soldiers and archers got killed, unless there was an accident or a mistake.

So knights were taught to regard war as enjoyable and exciting, and a young knight with no land of his own and no other duties would naturally be keen to try out his skill and prepare for the day when he might fight a battle. Such knights were the keenest supporters of tournaments, right from the earliest one we know of, which took place in 1066 in France. These first tournaments were simply a kind of imitation warfare. They were usually fought over a limited area, with weapons which had been blunted, but otherwise the armour and equipment were exactly like that used in a real war. The knight would wear a simple basin-shaped helmet with a piece on the front to protect his nose, and a tunic made of chain-mail which would stop a sword-blow. Underneath the tunic would be a jerkin to prevent the blow causing a bruise. He would have little protection on his legs and hands, but he would carry a long pointed shield. His weapons were a long lance and a big sword, sometimes used with both hands. His horse had no armour, and the saddle and stirrups were those used by an ordinary rider.

2 Tournament Rules

There were no real rules, and no referees. There was a retreat set aside for knights to withdraw from the fighting and repair their armour or harness, and there were supposed to be limits to the area over which the fighting took place. But knights often chased their opponents for miles, sometimes into a nearby town, so these were not very strictly kept to. There might be three or four teams of knights, each fighting on their own account and changing alliances in the middle of a battle. These teams were usually organized by local princes, who would have led an army in a real war. The main object was to capture knights and hold them and their equipment to ransom, and a successful fighter could make quite a lot of money out of his captures. William Marshal, who started as a penniless knight in Henry II's reign, made his early career in tournaments in the 1160s and 1170s and ended up as regent of England in Henry III's reign, in the 1220s. His biography tells us a lot about early tournaments. There was little idea of fair play. Philip of France used to wait on the sidelines until the other fighters were exhausted. Then he would come in and capture them when they were too tired to put up much resistance. Footsoldiers were sometimes used to capture knights, so that a knight who arrived with a hundred or so men-at-arms had a much better chance. This was unusual in France, where most tournaments were held, but it was common in Germany.

Early tournaments were dangerous, and knights were often killed. Also, they were so like real war that there was always a risk that they would turn into a rebellion or private feud. In England the kings succeeded in banning them as a danger to the peace. This ban was occasionally lifted after 1194, and in the fourteenth century, when tournaments had become more like games, the laws against them were ignored. Until then, English knights had to go to France to fight in tournaments. France became the centre for tournaments, and remained so until the sixteenth century.

3 Tournaments and Jousts

In the rough and tumble of an early tournament it was not often easy to tell who was the best fighter, and so besides the general battle or *mêlée*, it became the fashion to hold contests, called jousts, between just two knights. This made it easier for a good knight to win a reputation. One of the first to go in for jousting was a rather eccentric character, the poet Ulrich von Lichtenstein, who travelled through northern Italy and Austria in 1227, challenging all comers to fight with him in honour of the lady whom he loved.

In one month, Ulrich broke over three hundred spears; at least, that is what he tells us in his autobiography. If it is true, he must have been very good at jousting. The object was to ride straight at your opponent, holding your long wooden lance tightly so that it struck him firmly on the shield. If your aim was good and your grip firm, the impact would break the lance or unseat him. But it was a small target when you were moving at fifteen or twenty miles an hour, and it was hard to hold the lance as it struck your opponent. If either of the knights was unseated, or when three spears had been broken, the contest often continued on foot, with swords.

Jousts seem to have started in Germany, and they were only taken up in France and England later on. The tournament remained popular, particularly with onlookers, so the two forms were combined. Proceedings opened with a tournament proper, or *mêlée*, and then went on to the individual jousts. But even as late as Edward III's reign (1327–77) the tournament in its old form continued. He and his son the Black Prince were both enthusiasts when it came to tournaments.

By this time, however, the proper weapons of war were rarely used: the lances had a little attachment on the end, called a 'coronal' because it looked like a crown, which meant that the point would not go through a joint in the armour. The swords were usually 'rebated', blunted on both edges and at the point. These were called 'courtesy weapons'. On rare occasions knights went back to real weapons, in which case the jousts were *à outrance*, 'to the bitter end', though they were usually stopped before anyone was killed.

4 Preparing for a Tournament

We do not know a great deal about how tournaments were organized before the fifteenth century, because no one wrote down the rules. But about 1450, several noblemen who enjoyed tournaments recorded their versions of what happened. The most famous of these was René, duke of Anjou and Naples. He was born in 1409. After a none too successful military career – he was captured by the Burgundians in 1431 and was driven out of Naples in 1442 – he settled down to rule his lands along the river Loire and in the south of France. As a pastime, he held elaborate tournaments. Most of them had a complicated framework in which the

knights played different parts, as if in a play. For instance, a mysterious damsel would arrive at court and seek help. Some of the knights would go to her rescue, and the plot of their adventures would be organized so that it ended with the tournament. The tournament might be held for a particular occasion, a wedding or the knighting of a prince; and then the plot would be centred on the event in question. Even the fashion for pastoral poems, about shepherds and shepherdesses living a simple, carefree life, was used: René himself held a 'Passage of Arms of the Shepherdess' in 1449.

Strictly speaking, tournaments and 'passages of

arms' were slightly different. There were two ways of beginning the arrangements for a tournament. If you were a prince like René, you could send your heralds to another prince and challenge him to a tournament. The only trouble was that there were not many lords who could produce enough knights to make up one side in a tournament. So by the late fourteenth century, the passage of arms had become more usual. For a passage of arms, you simply announced through your herald that you and your knights were going to hold a particular place against all comers between certain dates. One of the earliest of these was organized by a French knight during a truce in the Hundred Years War. It was held near Calais and lasted for thirty days. Knights came from England, Spain, and Germany to challenge the French, and it was a great success.

Besides announcing the date and place of the event – an important task when there was no other way of spreading news – the heralds would organize the details. If it was to be a 'romantic' event, with a plot prepared beforehand, they would arrange who was to play different parts. During the proceedings they kept order and noted the jousting scores. They were also experts on coats of arms, and would know a knight by his shield when he was in the thick of the fighting. Later, knights would adopt special coats of arms or 'devices' for a particular tournament. These all had a special meaning, and the heralds would explain these to the watching ladies.

A Fifteenth-Century Tournament

5 The knights assemble

Tournaments were popular not only with the knights who took part but also with the ladies, courtiers and common people who gathered to watch. In London, they were often held at Smithfield, which was the place where London citizens went for amusement and exercise of all kinds,

rather like Wembley or the White City today. But there was no permanent stadium, and special seating and barriers had to be put up each time. The area in which the tournament was fought was known as the 'lists'. It was surrounded by a stout fence made of stakes driven into the ground. This in turn was surrounded by an even higher fence. The space between was used by the squires, heralds, and other attendants, who might have to rescue injured knights or give their masters new weapons. The whole area enclosed was perhaps 150 yards by 100 yards. Behind the fence were tiers of seats for the ladies and courtiers, while to one side the squires and ordinary people stood to watch.

Tournaments usually started on a Monday and continued till Thursday. If the event was to go on into the following week, there was then a break of three days, because Friday, Saturday, and Sunday were days when fighting was forbidden by the Church. The knights taking part in a tournament usually arrived two or three days beforehand to rest their horses and prepare themselves. Armour had to be unpacked and polished. New 'devices' or coats of arms for the tournament had to be made and painted. Horses might have to be reshod, and the elaborate horse-armour and long horse-cloths had to be prepared. Lances and swords had to be checked and, if need be, blunted.

The armour of a fifteenth-century knight was very complicated compared with the simple chain-mail and helmet of three hundred years before. It was made of overlapping iron plates, and had to be made to measure. The whole body was covered, and there were ingenious joints so that the knight could move freely. Even his hands were covered by jointed steel gloves, and he wore a heavy padded helmet, with a small moveable piece called a vizor. The vizor had slits in it, and he had to peer through these when it was closed. When he was not in the lists, he could lift the vizor; this made it easier to see – and to breathe! When a knight was in full armour with his vizor down, he was unrecognizable, and this was why coats of arms were painted on shields. It was the only way of telling who was inside.

6 Inspection of the banners

The right to take part in tournaments was jealously guarded. At a 'passage of arms', where knights might arrive from all over Europe, it was important to make sure that they were really knights. Medieval men thought of people's rank as something very important, which did not change. Only knights could take part in tournaments. So if you were an ambitious merchant's son, it was almost impossible to get in, even if you were very good at fighting. In case anyone tried there was a ceremony, usually two or three days before the tournament, when all the banners of the knights taking part were inspected by the heralds. In order to take part you had to belong to a family whose members were knights. If you were married, your wife had to be of equal rank. If you had broken your word or had lent money for interest, you would be banned; and if a lady saw your banner and complained that you had mistreated her, you would also be thrown out of the tournament. Your banner would be taken down, and you might even be held prisoner. The display of banners had another purpose as well: the spectators could look at the coats of arms, and this would help them to remember who was who in the fighting.

On the day before the tournament, usually a Sunday, the knights would attend a ceremony at which they swore to 'keep the peace', and not let the tournament develop into a kind of private war. (This had often happened in the past. Even Edward I once lost his temper at a French tournament at Châlons, and the resulting battle was known as 'the Little War of Châlons'.) Then the ladies would choose a 'knight of honour' to open the tournament.

7 The start of the tournament

On the opening day of the tournament the knights assembled in the lists and the ladies took up their places in the stands. Before the fighting started there might well be a little piece of pageantry, if the 'passage of arms' had a romantic plot. The damsel who was supposed to have been wronged would appear and put her complaint to the king or the judges who presided over the tournament. Her enemies would form one team of knights, her rescuers the other. Or the two sides might simply be the retinues or followers of two great lords. They lined up in the lists, separated by cords tied across between the fences.

The heralds would read the rules of the tournament, and warn the knights not to give unfair blows and not to go on fighting when the signal to stop had been given. Then the knight of honour cut the cords, and the fighting or *mêlée* began. The lances used in the first charge would be quickly broken or thrown aside. Then the knights drew

their swords – blunted, of course – and fought on horseback with these. Any knights who were unseated could remount, and their squires could help them. Indeed, few knights could get back on their horses wearing full armour unless they were helped. The squires were allowed to wear armour, but not to carry weapons. Otherwise they might have been tempted to join in the fighting. Some knights might get tired, in which case they could retire to the space between the two fences where the squires stood. When they had recovered, they could return to the fighting.

The tournament would go on from about one o'clock until dark. Sometimes torches would be lit, and fighting would continue in the dark until the heralds raised their silver trumpets and blew the signal for the general retreat. Then everyone went to their lodgings, to rest or to prepare for the dance that evening. At the dance, prizes for the best performances of the day were given, and details of the next day's jousts announced.

8 The jousts

The jousts were the most exciting part of the tournament, rather like a modern tennis or golf championship. The lists were arranged slightly differently: a wooden barrier was built down the centre, so that the two knights did not collide if one of the horses swerved. Originally the jousting was with spears only, and this remained the most important part. There was a carefully worked out system of scoring. The greatest feat was to unhorse another knight. After this came striking your opponent's spear on the tip or 'coronal': to do this twice qualified a knight for the prize, if no one had been unhorsed. Then came striking your opponent three times on the crest of his helm (in separate jousts). Breaking the spear only counted if none of the previous feats had been performed. But there

were also penalties: striking the barrier or your opponent's saddle meant that one spear was taken off your total of spears broken; while striking a horse meant that you were instantly disqualified. There was even a ban on a particular piece of armour, a special gauntlet which locked on to the spear and gave a perfect grip! Scorecards or 'jousting cheques' from Henry VIII's court still survive; they have been marked up according to these rules. The jousts with spears were sometimes followed by swordplay on horseback (see spread 9), with the barriers still in place. Here there was no simple system of scoring. It was a matter of endurance rather than skill, as you were unlikely to unseat your opponent.

10 Fighting on foot

Either on the same day as the jousts on horseback, or as a separate event, there would be foot-combats. Sometimes these followed on immediately after two knights had run three 'courses' with spears on horseback, so that it became a kind of duel with changes of weapons at intervals. Once again, there was no system of scoring, though judges might award prizes on their opinion of the two fighters. It is difficult to tell how a challenge like this one issued in 1442 could be settled, unless the knights fought until one was exhausted or his armour too badly damaged to continue. The terms of the challenge run:

We shall fight on horseback, both armed as we please, with the usual weapons of battle, namely spears, swords

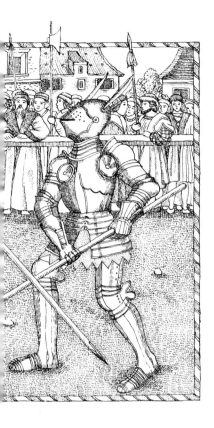

and daggers, and with such equipment as either of us wish, without any trickery.

He to whom God gives the victory shall have the other's sword and helm or other head-armour.

If the said battle does not end on the same day, we shall complete it on foot without any repairs or replacements.

Wrestling with legs and feet, arms and hands shall be allowed.

A picture of a joust at Smithfield in 1466 shows one of the combatants being wounded; the king, presiding over the jousts, is about to throw down his baton to stop the contest. Such individual challenges became common for a time in the fifteenth century. However, it was at the court of Maximilian I, emperor of Germany from 1486 to 1519, that the fighting on foot became most elaborate.

11 Feasts and Dancing

Both during the tournament – if it went on for several days – and at the end, there would be feasts and dancing each evening. For tournaments were great social occasions, times when ladies wanted to show off their finery just as much as knights wanted to show off their skill. In the early days of tournaments, in the twelfth century, there had been less of this: a minstrel or two might turn up to entertain the knights before or after the fighting, but it was all quite informal. In the 1170s, William Marshal, whom we have already met (see spread 2), went to a tournament at Joigny. There was no minstrel, but William sang instead, so that the others could dance, and everyone was full of admiration. When a minstrel arrived, he made up a ballad with the refrain 'Marshal, give me a horse', implying that if knights had taken over the minstrel's job, the minstrel had better go and fight. William earned even more applause by presenting the first horse he won in the lists to the minstrel.

This free-and-easy atmosphere became much more formal by the fifteenth century. The minstrels had always encouraged knights to be generous, holding up to scorn anyone who was mean. But

now only a prince could afford generosity (or *largesse*) on the scale that was needed. The feasts could be incredibly lavish: a feast given in Milan in 1368 for the wedding of Edward III's son to the daughter of the Duke ran to eighteen courses, sixteen of which were fish and meat, with junket, cheese, and fruit as the last two. Of course this was an important state occasion, but the guests at a tournament would have done almost as well.

After the feast there would be entertainments and dancing. The entertainments might be a kind of play or pantomime, often with a hidden meaning. Such hidden meanings or allegories were very popular at the time. When the message finally became clear, it was usually in praise of whoever was holding the tournament, or it was designed as propaganda for some political plan. This was because princes did not always hold tournaments just because they enjoyed them. A prince was expected to spend lavishly – it was how a prince was meant to behave. But if he could also use such occasions to achieve other ends – to win new allies or undermine his enemies' schemes – he would certainly do so.

During the evening, the prizes for the best knight in the tournament would be given. These were usually jewels, which both men and women wore, and which were a valuable kind of money in those days. It was only in romances that the best knight won a beautiful lady's hand!

12 Armour for Tournaments

In many tournaments the armour used was the same as that for war. But just as weapons were adapted for tournaments so armour also was specially made. A list of armour for a tournament held by Edward I at Windsor in 1278 mentions leather helmets and whalebone swords. These were evidently replicas of ordinary armour, and only the materials from which they were made were different. By 1400, the special rules of jousting had led to purpose-built helmets being made. These were so designed that the knight could only see when he was leaning forward, as he would do when he spurred his horse forward at the beginning of a joust. When he leaned back, at the moment when he made contact with his opponent, he could see nothing, but his face was completely protected. This helmet design was so successful that it was used for nearly a hundred and fifty years for jousting. Other special pieces, mostly designed as extra protection, included one which covered the left

arm but allowed very little movement. Saddles were also adapted, and often had large protective pieces for the rider's legs built on to them, so that the knight did not need leg-armour.

In Germany, the joust became very complicated, with subdivisions and special rules; in one type, the object was to unseat your opponent, in another it was to break lances, and in yet another it was to hit your opponent's shield exactly in the middle. Each had its special equipment. The 'high seat jousts' needed a kind of wooden cage on the saddle, which held the knight in a standing position by means of a raised seat and a wooden frame behind

his back. Armour for the simplest type of joust had special rests for the lance, a kind of bracket on the right hand side by the hip, under which the butt end fitted. For the *Mechanical Joust* invented by the Emperor Maximilian, a spring-loaded shield was used. If you struck in the middle, the springs were released and the shield flew apart in wedge-shaped pieces.

Most spectacular of all were the richly gilded and decorated suits of parade armour, used only for show. These suits were often of extraordinary design: the Emperor Charles V had one which was supposed to be a copy of Roman armour.

Because armour was very expensive, and the basic design of armour for real war and for tournaments was not very different, armourers designed complete sets which had interchangeable pieces. One such set, made in 1547 for an Austrian duke, has over sixty pieces all with the same decorative pattern of eagles, and makes up into three kinds of tournament armour and five kinds of armour for war. It includes a locking gauntlet, which locked the sword or spear into the wearer's grip: this was banned in tournaments, but was a great advantage in a real battle.

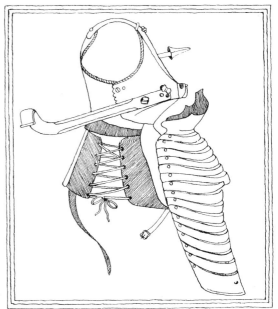

13 Tournaments under the Tudors

Henry VIII was famous as a jouster in the early years of his reign, and his enthusiasm led him to spend over £4000 on a single tournament held at Westminster in 1511 to celebrate the birth of Prince Arthur. The largest warship in his navy cost only £2300, so it was a very expensive event indeed. It was all recorded in a richly illustrated manuscript, *The Great Tournament Roll of Westminster*. Naturally, when he met Francis I of France at the Field of the Cloth of Gold four years later,

there were plans for a great tournament among the entertainments. With 3000 lances provided for the English knights alone, preparations were on a lavish scale. However, these were spoilt by wind and rain and, although the jousting took place, it was not the splendid occasion it should have been.

Tournaments disappeared from England during the later years of Henry VIII's reign, and were not revived for fifty years or more. The next tournament of which there is a record is one held

in honour of Queen Elizabeth I, on the twenty-third anniversary of her coming to the throne. It became an annual event, and the anniversary was kept as a holiday, called 'Accession Day'.

A special cult in poetry and art had grown up around Elizabeth who was called 'Oriana' or 'the Virgin Queen'. The Accession Day tournaments had elaborate 'plots' which reflected this hero-worship of the Queen. The knights carried devices on their shields which all had hidden meanings. In 1587, these were so complicated that they had to be carefully explained in a booklet handed out to the spectators.

The jousts, or 'tilts' as they were now called, differed little from those of the fifteenth century. The death of Henri II of France in a jousting accident in 1559 had underlined the dangers of the sport. His opponent, the Count de Montgomeri, had failed to drop the splintered end of a broken lance, which went through the king's vizor. At Elizabeth's court the actual jousting seems to have been largely a ritual, and the real attention focused on the ceremonies. The Accession Day tilts did not long survive 'Oriana's' death in 1603. Henry Prince of Wales, James I's eldest son, was an enthusiast, but he died in 1612. The last such tilts were held in 1621.

14 The Last Tournaments

Outside England, tournaments continued in different forms until the end of the seventeenth century. But after 1600, when the lance began to go out of use in real warfare, they became completely without any kind of value as training for soldiers. Furthermore, as the seventeenth century progressed, armour was gradually abandoned. This was because the new guns of the time were powerful enough to send a bullet through any kind of armour that could be worn with reasonable ease. Pistols and swords were now the cavalry weapons, and ease of movement was more important than protection against a sword-thrust. So the fully-armed knights gave way to the partly-armed cuirassiers, wearing only breastplates and helmets. By the end of the seventeenth century, the British regiments had returned their armour to the Tower armouries for storage; the last armourer died in the mid-eighteenth century.

So tournaments became curiosities, something from the past. In Italy and France the jousting was replaced by displays of horsemanship or 'carrousels'. Some of the means by which knights had trained in the old days were brought into these displays. In particular, riding at the quintain, a kind of tilting target, was revived. The quintain consisted of an arm revolving on a post: the object was to hit the arm squarely and make it rotate. This needed all the skill of a real joust, except that of meeting the impact of the other rider's lance. But it was far less dangerous. The only hazard was that if you rode too slowly, the other end of the arm would catch you on the back of the head as you went by.

One last tournament deserves a mention. In 1839, Lord Eglinton and some friends decided to hold a tournament. No expense was spared to get details right and to provide a magnificent spectacle. Sir Walter Scott's novels were all the rage, and this was to rival the tournaments Scott described in *Ivanhoe*. But the noble lords found that jousting was not an art that could be learnt in a month or two. Only two of the knights were even passable in the lists. The real disaster was the weather: instead of the brilliant pageant planned, it was a sodden, wind-swept gathering. Organized on a vast scale, it was too expensive to repeat: so the 'last tournament' ended with the sorry sight of unsteady riders floundering through mud and finally missing each other altogether.

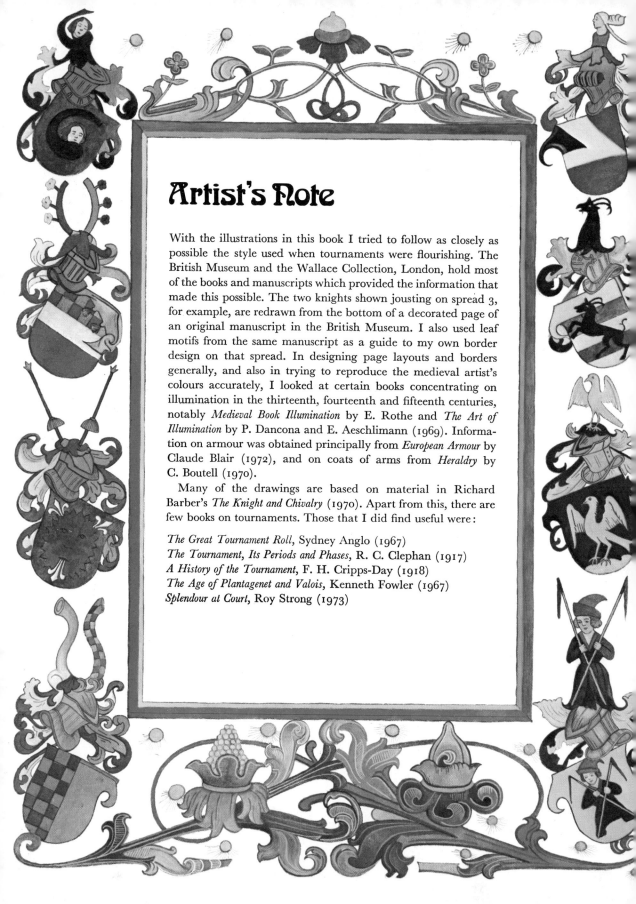

Artist's Note

With the illustrations in this book I tried to follow as closely as possible the style used when tournaments were flourishing. The British Museum and the Wallace Collection, London, hold most of the books and manuscripts which provided the information that made this possible. The two knights shown jousting on spread 3, for example, are redrawn from the bottom of a decorated page of an original manuscript in the British Museum. I also used leaf motifs from the same manuscript as a guide to my own border design on that spread. In designing page layouts and borders generally, and also in trying to reproduce the medieval artist's colours accurately, I looked at certain books concentrating on illumination in the thirteenth, fourteenth and fifteenth centuries, notably *Medieval Book Illumination* by E. Rothe and *The Art of Illumination* by P. Dancona and E. Aeschlimann (1969). Information on armour was obtained principally from *European Armour* by Claude Blair (1972), and on coats of arms from *Heraldry* by C. Boutell (1970).

Many of the drawings are based on material in Richard Barber's *The Knight and Chivalry* (1970). Apart from this, there are few books on tournaments. Those that I did find useful were:

The Great Tournament Roll, Sydney Anglo (1967)
The Tournament, Its Periods and Phases, R. C. Clephan (1917)
A History of the Tournament, F. H. Cripps-Day (1918)
The Age of Plantagenet and Valois, Kenneth Fowler (1967)
Splendour at Court, Roy Strong (1973)